THEODORE ROOSEVELT
NATIONAL PARK
ACTIVITY BOOK

PUZZLES, MAZES, GAMES, AND MORE ABOUT
THEODORE ROOSEVELT NATIONAL PARK

NATIONAL PARKS ACTIVITIES SERIES

THEODORE ROOSEVELT
NATIONAL PARK
ACTIVITY BOOK

Copyright 2022
Published by Little Bison Press

The author acknowledges that the land on which Theodore Roosevelt National Park is located are the traditional lands of the Mandan, Hidatsa, and Crow Tribes as well as other Indigenous peoples.

LITTLE BISON

Press

For more free national parks activities, visit
Littlebisonpress.com

About Theodore Roosevelt National Park

Theodore Roosevelt National Park is located in the state of North Dakota. The park's namesake is the 26th President of the United States who spent many formative years in what is now the national park. Theodore first visited North Dakota to hunt bison when he was 24 years old but fell in love with the area. His time there greatly influenced his work as president to protect wildlife and public lands. You can learn more about his life and the time he spent in North Dakota if you visit the South Unit Visitor Center near the town of Medora.

The park encompasses over 70,000 acres of colorful canyons, beautiful badlands, snaking rivers, and a diverse array of wildlife. Both the North and South units of the park provide breathtaking scenic drives. Hiking, fishing, and bird watching are popular activities in the park.

Visitors can visit The Elkhorn Ranch Unit of the park. The 218-acre site preserves Theodore Roosevelt's "main ranch", which was built in 1884 on the banks of the Little Missouri River. Exhibits feature passages written by Roosevelt about his experiences at the ranch.

Theodore Roosevelt National Park is famous for:
- prairies, canyons, badlands, and rivers
- prairie dog towns
- The Elkhorn Ranch

Hey! I'm Parker!

I'm the only snail in history to visit every National Park in the United States! Come join me on my adventures in Theodore Roosevelt National Park.

Throughout this book, we will learn about the history of the park, the animals and plants that live here, and things to do here if you ever get to visit in person. This book is also full of games and activities!

Last but not least, I am hidden 9 times on different pages. See how many times you can find me. This page doesn't count!

Theodore Roosevelt Bingo

Let's play bingo! Cross off each box that you are able to during your visit to the national park. Try to get a bingo down, across, or diagonally. If you can't visit the park, use the bingo board to plan your perfect trip.

Pick out some activities that you would want to do during your visit. What would you do first? How long would you spend there? What animals would you try to see?

SPOT A BISON	VISIT THE MALTESE CROSS CABIN	GO FOR A HIKE	TAKE A PICTURE AT AN OVERLOOK	WATCH A MOVIE AT THE VISITORS CENTER
IDENTIFY A TREE	LEARN ABOUT THE INDIGENOUS PEOPLE THAT LIVE IN THIS AREA	WITNESS A SUNRISE OR SUNSET	OBSERVE THE NIGHT SKIES	GO SNOWSHOEING
HEAR A BIRD CALL	SPOT A RIVER	FREE SPACE	LEARN ABOUT PRAIRIE DOGS	SPOT SOME ANIMAL TRACKS
PICK UP TEN PIECES OF TRASH	HAVE A PICNIC	SEE A MULE DEER	VISIT ELKHORN RANCH	SPOT A BIRD OF PREY
LEARN ABOUT THE GEOLOGY OF THE BADLANDS	SEE SOMEONE RIDING A HORSE	GO CAMPING	VISIT A RANGER STATION	PARTICIPATE IN A RANGER-LED ACTIVITY

The Beautiful Badlands

People come from all over the world to check out the unique layers of the badlands at Theodore Roosevelt National Park. If you are able to see the badlands for yourself, make some observations.

Draw or describe them in the boxes below, using lots of detail.

Something colorful	A unique rock	Something that moves
An insect	Something cool you saw	A tiny plant
Something with a smell	A leaf	Something shiny

Sensory Hike

Go for a sensory hike with your friends or family. Circle one activity from each sense to do along the way.

SEE

Stand in the prairie. What do you think lives here based on what you see?

OR

Look for tracks, scat (poop), or other evidence of animals on the trail. Who was on the trail before you?

SMELL

Take a deep breath in three different spots on your hike. Do they smell different? Why or why not?

OR

Take notice of any strong smells you encounter. Do they smell good, bad, or somewhere in between?

HEAR

Listen to a bird sound. What do you think its call or song says?

OR

Listen to the wind in the grasses. What sound does it make?

TOUCH

Try to find something with a rough surface and something with a smooth surface. Why do they feel different?

OR

Sit still on the ground for a few minutes and pretend you are a baby bison. What do you feel on the ground?

Which one was your favorite one to do? How did it make you feel?

_____

_____

_____

Rain, Rain, Rain

If it rains while you are visiting Theodore Roosevelt National Park, you can do this activity during your trip. If you don't get any rain while you are there, you can follow the same instructions next time it rains where you live.

Go outside into the rain. Use all of your senses as you complete the boxes below. You can use words, drawings, or both.

Sit as still as you can and listen to the rain. How does it make you feel?

Look straight up at the sky and let the raindrops fall on your face. Close your eyes. How does it feel?

Watch where the rain goes. Pay attention to the different surfaces the rain lands on. Which surfaces absorb the rain, and which surfaces cause the rain to run off or pool?

Are there any animals or bugs ou- enjoying the rain? Do you think the plants are enjoying the rain?

Go Horseback Riding on the Jones Creek Trail

Help find the horse's lost shoe!

start here →

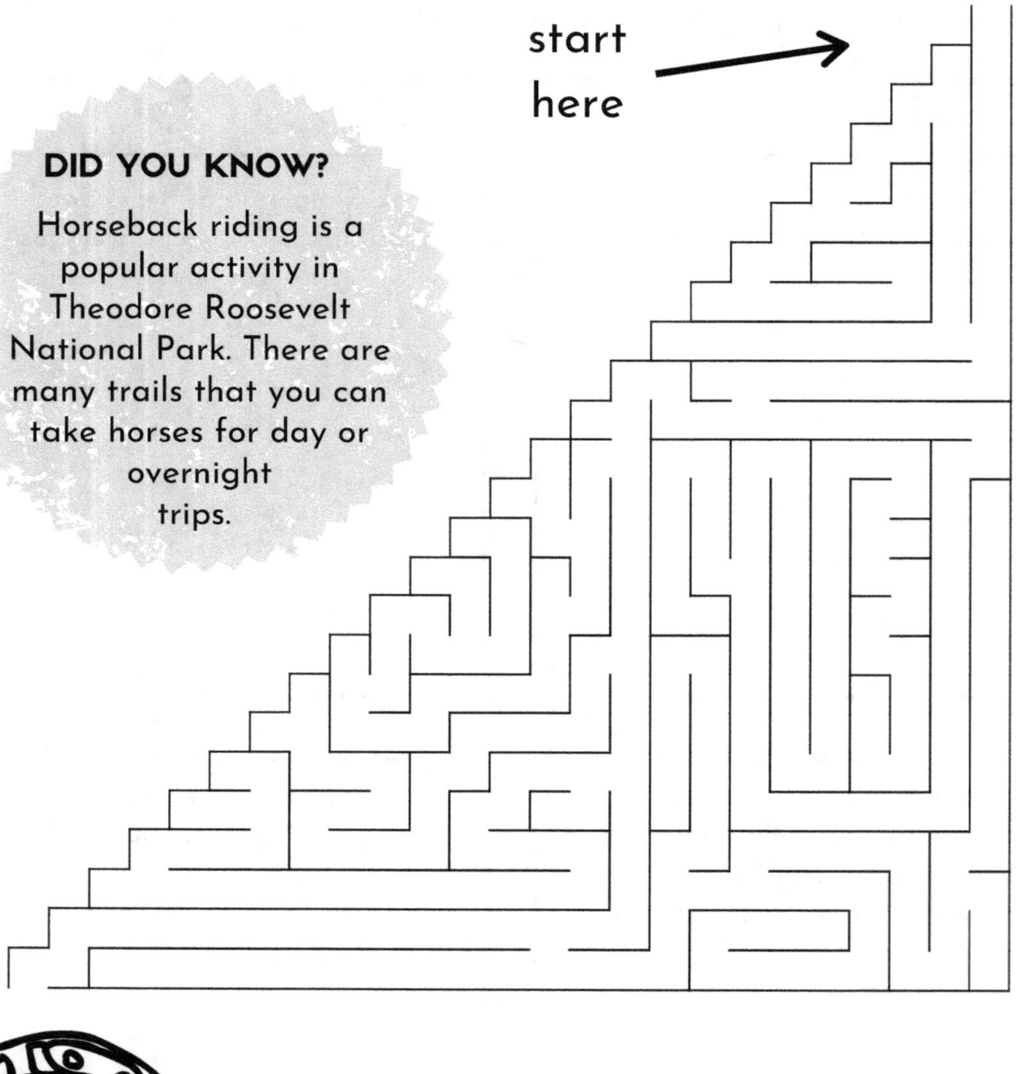

DID YOU KNOW?

Horseback riding is a popular activity in Theodore Roosevelt National Park. There are many trails that you can take horses for day or overnight trips.

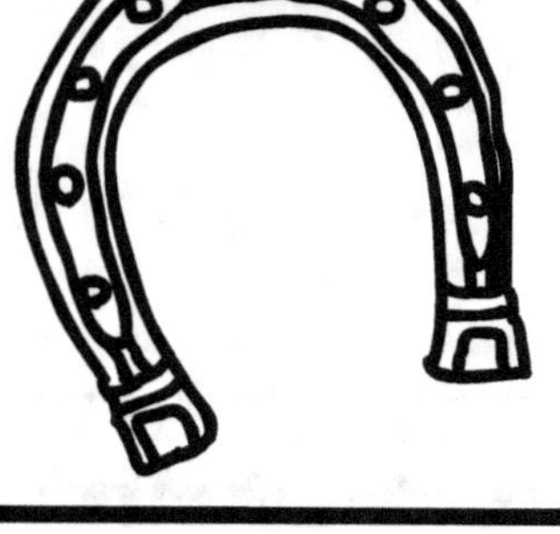

Bird Scavenger Hunt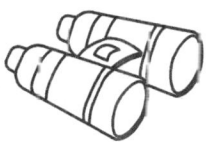

Theodore Roosevelt National Park is a great place to go birdwatching. You don't have to be able to identify different species of birds in order to have fun. Open your eyes and tune in your ears. Check off as many birds on this list as you can.

- [ ] A colorful bird
- [ ] A brown bird
- [ ] A bird in a tree
- [ ] A bird with long tail feathers
- [ ] A bird making noise
- [ ] A bird eating or hunting
- [ ] A bird with spots

- [ ] A big bird
- [ ] A small bird
- [ ] A hopping bird
- [ ] A flying bird
- [ ] A bird's nest
- [ ] A bird's footprint on the ground
- [ ] A bird with stripes somewhere on it

What was the easiest bird on the list to find? What was the hardest?
Why do you think that was?

_____

_____

_____

Theodore Roosevelt National Park

Date: _____   Season: _____

Who I went with: _____   Which entrance: _____

How was your experience? Write a few sentences on your trip. Where did you stay? What did you do? What was your favorite activity? If you have not yet visited the park, write a paragraph pretending that you did.

_____

_____

_____

_____

_____

STAMPS

Many national parks and monuments have cancellation stamps for visitors to use. These rubber stamps record the date and the location that you visited. Many people collect the markings as a free souvenir. Check with a ranger to see where you can find a stamp during your visit. If you aren't able to find one, you can draw your own.

Where is the Park?

Theodore Roosevelt National Park is in the Great Plains region of the United States. It is located in North Dakota, a state that shares a border with the country of Canada.

North Dakota

Look at the shape of North Dakota. Can you find it on the map? If you are from the US, can you find your home state? Color North Dakota red. Put a star on the map where you live.

Connect the Dots #1

Connect the dots to figure out what this tiny critter is. One species of these lives in Theodore Roosevelt National Park.

Their heart rate can reach as high as 1,260 beats per minute and a breathing rate of 250 breaths per minute. Have you ever measured your breathing rate? Ask a friend or family member to set a timer for 60 seconds. Once they say "go", try to breathe normally. Count each breath until they say "stop." How do your breaths per minute compare to hummingbirds?

_____

_____

The Prairie Rattlesnake is the only venomous reptile in Theodore Roosevelt Park. It is best known for the unique rings on the end of its tail that knock together and make a rattling sound.

American Bison are the largest surviving terrestrial animals in North America. Although commonly referred to as a buffalo in the United States and Canada, it is only distantly related to the true buffalo.

Who lives here?

Here are nine plants and animals that live in the park.
Use the word bank to fill in the clues below.

WORD BANK: COYOTE, SALAMANDER, BISON, PRAIRIE DOG, RATTLESNAKE, WILD TURKEY, PRONGHORN, ELK, POISON IVY

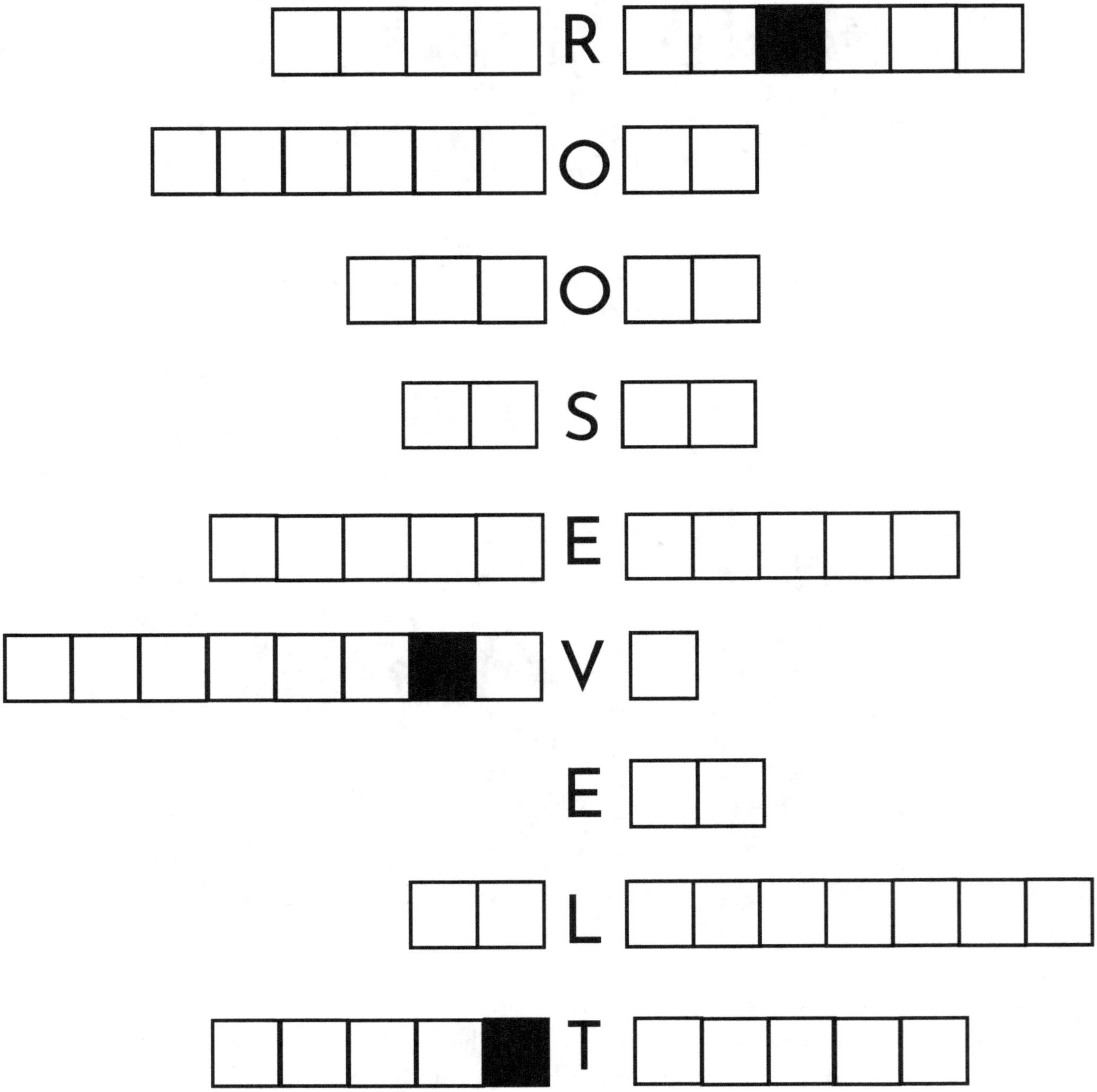

☐☐☐☐ R ☐☐■☐☐

☐☐☐☐☐☐ O ☐☐

☐☐☐ O ☐☐

☐☐ S ☐☐

☐☐☐☐☐ E ☐☐☐☐☐

☐☐☐☐☐■☐ V ☐

E ☐☐

☐☐ L ☐☐☐☐☐☐☐

☐☐☐☐■ T ☐☐☐☐☐

14

Turkeys don't just gobble, they make all kinds of sounds, including clucks and purrs and a cackle when they fly!

Black-tailed prairie dogs are small, short-tailed animals with eyes and small ears set far back on their heads. Head to the South Unit of the park to get a good view of the prairie dog towns!

Common Names
vs.
Scientific Names

A common name of an organism is a name that is based on everyday language. You have heard the common names of plants, animals, and other living things on tv, in books, and at school. Common names can also be referred to as "English" names, popular names, or farmer's name. Common names can vary from place to place. The word for a particular tree may be one thing, but that same tree has a different name in another country. Common names can even vary from region to region, even in the same country.

Scientific names, or Latin names, are given to organisms to make it possible to have uniform names for the same species. Scientific names are in Latin. You may have heard plants or animals referred to by their scientific name or at least parts of their scientific names. Latin names are also called "binomial nomenclature" which refers to a two-part naming system. The first part of the name - the generic name -names the genus to which the species belongs. The second part of the name, the specific name, identifies the species. For example, Tyrannosaurus rex is an example of a widely known scientific name.

Coyote

Canis latrans

COMMON NAME

Elk

Cervus canadensis

LATIN NAME = GENUS + SPECIES

Elk = Cervus canadensis

Coyote = Canis latrans

Find the Match!
Common Names and Latin Names

Match the common name to the scientific name for each animal. The first one is done for you. Use clues on the page before and after this one to complete the matches.

Pronghorn	Haliaeetus leucocephalus
Water Plantain	Ovis canadensis
Plains Bluegrass	Picoides villosus
Bighorn Sheep	Mustela nigripes
Great Horned Owl	Alisma triviale
Bald Eagle	Crotalus viridis
Hairy Woodpecker	Bubo virginianus
Black-footed Ferret	Antilcapra americana
Prairie Rattlesnake	Poa arida

Bald Eagle

Haliaeetus leucocephalus

Black-footed Ferret
Mustela nigripes

Bald Eagle
Haliaeetus leucocephalus

Great Horned Owl
Bubo virginianus

Some plants and animals that live at Theodore Roosevelt NP

Plains Bluegrass
Poa arida

Bighorn Sheep
Ovis canadensis

Prairie Rattlesnake
Crotalus viridis

Things to Do Jumble

Unscramble the letters to uncover activities you can do while in Theodore Roosevelt National Park. Hint: each one ends in -ing.

1. HFIS ☐☐☐☐ ING

2. KIH ☐☐☐ ING

3. IRBD ☐☐☐☐ ING

4. MACP ☐☐☐☐ ING

5. KINICPC ☐☐☐☐☐☐☐ ING

6. EISSTEHG ☐☐☐☐☐☐☐☐ ING

7. SARTGZA ☐☐☐☐☐☐☐ ING

Word Bank

birding
fishing
camping
stargazing
horseback riding
hiking
hunting
singing
yelling
sightseeing
picnicking

The National Park Logo

The National Park System has over 400 units in the US. Just like Theodore Roosevelt National Park, each location is unique or special in some way. The areas include other national parks, historic sites, monuments, seashores, and other recreation areas.

Each element of the National Park emblem represents something that the National Park Service protects. Fill in each blank below to show what each symbol represents.

WORD BANK:
MOUNTAINS, ARROWHEAD, BISON, SEQUOIA TREE, WATER

This represents all plants. _____

This represents all animals. _____

This symbol represents the landscapes. _____

This represents the waters protected by the park service. _____

This represents the historical and archeological values. _____

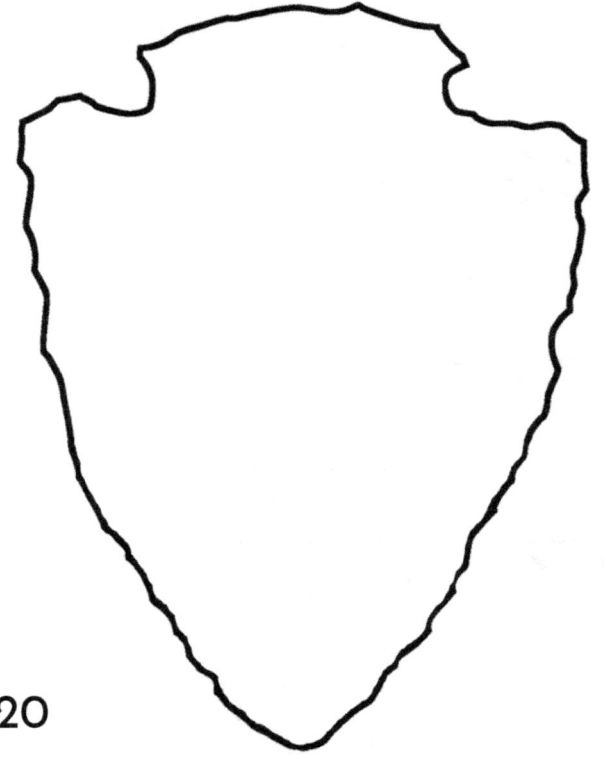

Now it's your turn! Pretend you are designing a new national park. Add elements to the design that represent the things that your park protects

What is the name of your park?

Describe why you included the symbols that you included. What do they mean?

The Ten Essentials

The ten essentials is a list of things that are important to have when you go for longer hikes. If you go on a hike to the <u>backcountry</u>, it is especially important that you have everything you need in case of an emergency. If you get lost or something unforeseen happens, it is good to be prepared to survive until help finds you.

The ten essentials list was developed in the 1930s by an outdoors group called the Mountaineers. Over time and technological advancements, this list has evolved. Can you identify all the things on the current list? Circle each of the "essentials" and cross out everything that doesn't make the cut.

fire: matches, lighter, tinder and/or stove	a pint of milk	extra money	headlamp plus extra batteries	extra clothes
extra water	a dog	Polaroid camera	bug net	lightweight games, like a deck of cards
extra food	a roll of duct tape	shelter	sun protection like sunglasses, sun-protective clothes and sunscreen	knife: plus a gear repair kit
a mirror	navigation: map, compass, altimeter, GPS device, or satellite messenger	first aid kit	extra flip-flops	entertainment like video games or books

Backcountry- a remote undeveloped rural area.

Connect the Dots #2

This animal lives in almost every state in the US, including the national park. They are nocturnal and are more active at night and sleep during the day. They are omnivorous eaters, which means they eat both plants and animals.

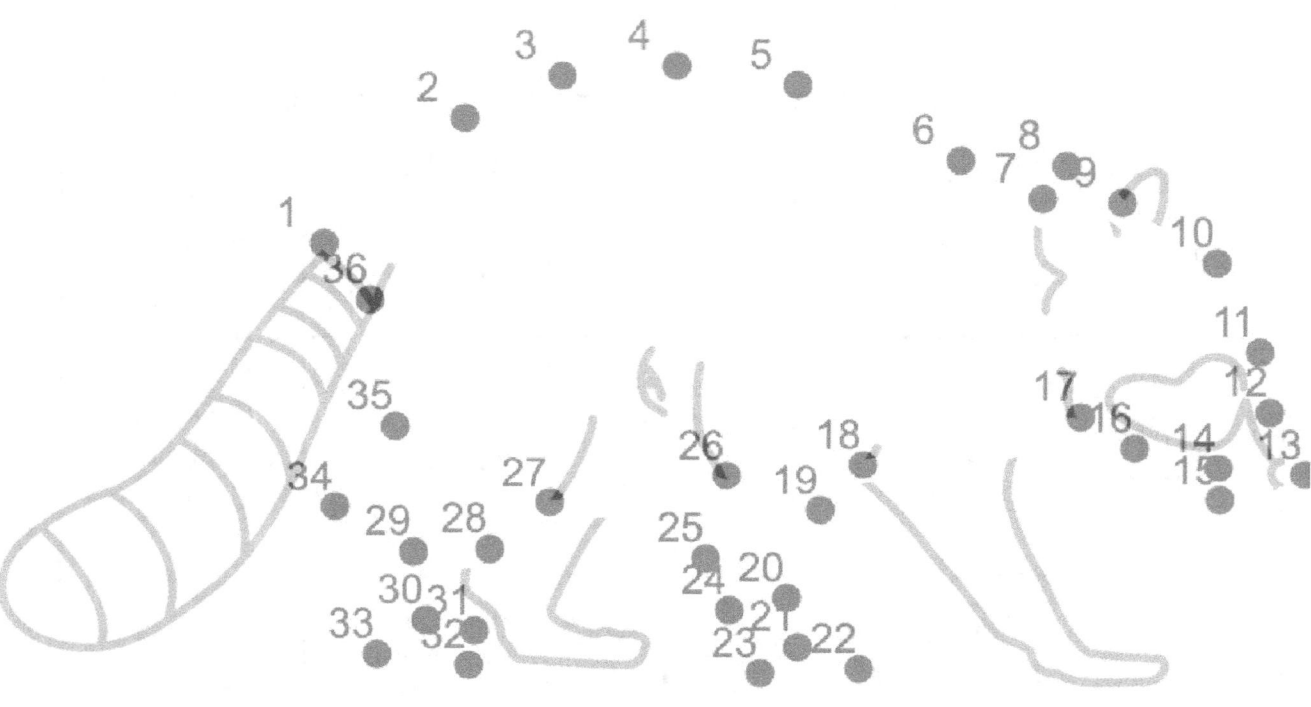

Are you an omnivore like a raccoon? An herbivore only eats plant foods. A carnivore only eats meat. An omnivore eats both. What type of eater are you? Write down some of your favorite foods to back up your answer.

_____

_____

Prairie Dog Digs

Prairie dog colonies or "towns" are made up of tunnels 3 to 6 feet below ground and about 15 feet long. These burrows usually include several distinct chambers inhabited by a coterie, or group, of prairie dogs. These coteries work together to protect the group from predators like coyotes, badgers, birds of prey, and the black-footed ferret. Prairie dog burrows have areas dug out for raising babies, sleeping, and even toilets. They also feature dugouts near the exits, so the prairie dogs can listen to potential predators outside.

Using your knowledge of prairie dog habitat, draw your own version of a prairie dog burrow. Your drawing should include at least 3 different chambers, a coterie with at least 4 prairie dogs, and one potential predator waiting on the surface.

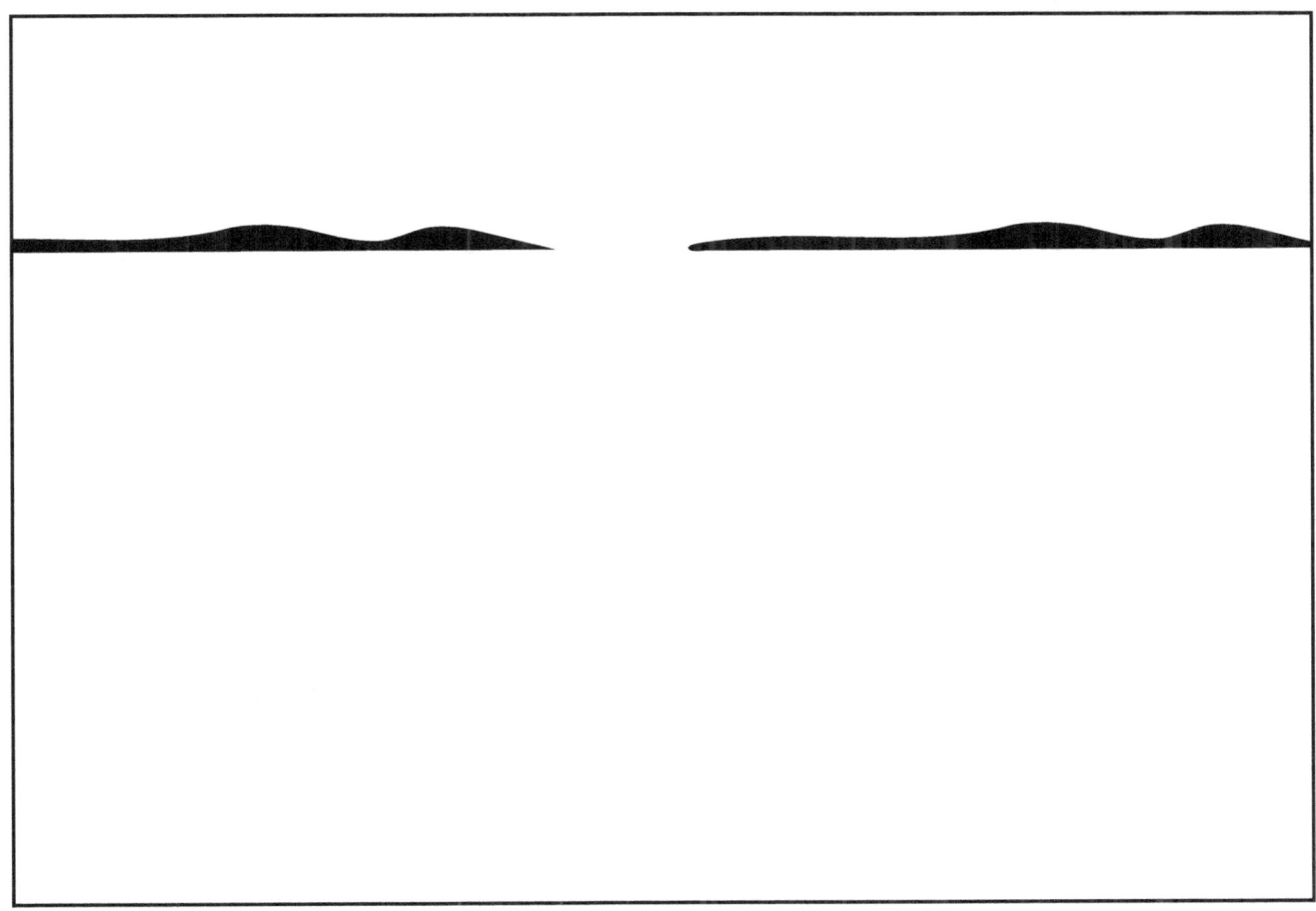

Which predator of the prairie dog did you draw? Do you think it will be able to successfully hunt any members of your coterie?

_____

_____

_____

Camping Packing List

What should you take with you camping? Pretend you are in charge of your family camping trip. Make a list of what you would need to be safe and comfortable on an overnight excursion. Some considerations are listed on the side.

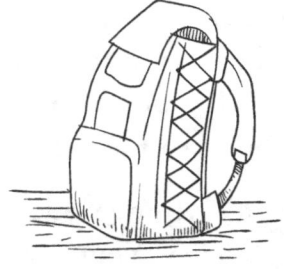

1.
2.
3.
4.
5.
6.
7.
8.
9.
10.
11.
12.
13.
14.
15.
16.

- What will you eat at every meal?

- What will the weather be like?

- Where will you sleep?

- What will you do during your free time?

- How luxurious do you want camp to be?

- How will you cook?

- How will you see at night?

- How will you dispose of trash?

- What might you need in case of emergencies?

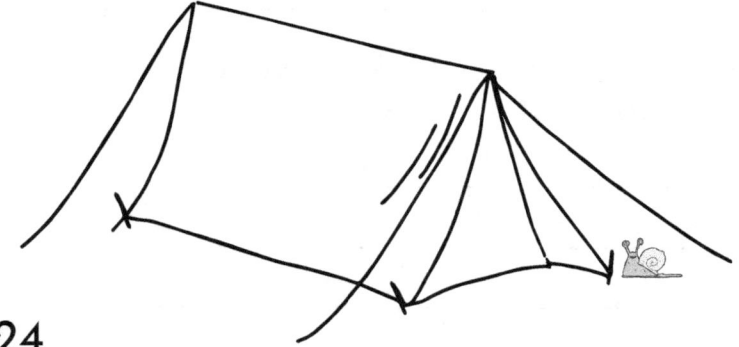

Theodore Roosevelt National Park has two regular campgrounds and one place where you can camp with horses!

Theodore Roosevelt Word Search

Words may be horizontal, vertical, or diagonal
and they might be backward!

1. bison
2. badlands
3. Teddy
4. North Dakota
5. ranch
6. cabin
7. horse
8. rattlesnakes
9. Peck Hill
10. conservation
11. camp ground
12. prairie dogs
13. oil boom
14. maltese
15. sagebrush
16. snapping turtle

```
C W O I L B O O M S K L O W K
H T A S C I L O C H E H A E J
T E P R O A O S B I S O N L D
S M P A N P R S C D R R U T N
C Y A D S A B L N E I S J R U
A D E S E T L A M C T E A U O
R E S T R H L K I N K R I T R
P E B A V D I E G W N E K G G
A T O K A D H T R O N D Y N P
E C I B T B O Y A I P G O I M
Q T A H I H I N N O K E N P A
S R N I O O E I C A B I N P C
I I O S N Z I R H I C A L A W
J S P E C K H I L L O R V N H
N I C A K M S A G E B R U S H
R A T T L E S N A K E S Q N L
H Y P R A I R I E D O G S E E
C J D O S N E D N Y M A L A M
```

Wildlife Wisdom

The national park is home to a lot of different kinds of animals. Seeing wildlife can be an exciting thing about visiting the national park but it is important to remember that these animals are wild. They need plenty of space and a healthy habitat where they can find their own food. Part of this is not allowing animals to eat any human food. This is their home and we are the visitors. We need to be respectful of the wildlife in the park.

Directions: Circle the highlighted words that best complete the following sentences.

If an animal changes its behavior because of your presence, you are:
A) too close
B) funny looking
C) dehydrated and should drink more water

The best thing we can do to help wild animals survive is:
A) make them pets
B) protect their habitat
C) knit them winter sweaters

In a national park, it is okay to share your food with wild animals:
A) never
B) always
C) sometimes

When you're hiking in an area where there are bears, you should warn bears that you are entering their space by:
A) hiking quietly
B) making noise
C) wearing bright colors

At night, park rangers care for the animals by:
A) putting them back into their cages
B) tucking them into bed
C) leaving them alone

If you see an abandoned bird's nest, it is best to:
A) pet the baby birds
B) leave it alone
C) crunch the empty eggshells

Bears look under logs in hopes of finding:
A) granola bars
B) insects
C) peanuts to eat

The place where an animal lives is called its
A) condo
B) habitat
C) crib

Color the badlands.

The Perfect Picnic Spot

Fill in the blanks on this page without looking at the full story. Once you have each line filled out, use the words you've chosen to complete the story on the next page.

EMOTION _____

FOOD _____

SOMETHING SWEET _____

STORE _____

MODE OF TRANSPORTATION _____

NOUN _____

SOMETHING ALIVE _____

SAUCE _____

PLURAL VEGETABLES _____

ADJECTIVE _____

PLURAL BODY PART _____

ANIMAL _____

PLURAL FRUIT _____

PLACE _____

SOMETHING TALL _____

COLOR _____

ADJECTIVE _____

NOUN _____

A DIFFERENT ANIMAL _____

FAMILY MEMBER #1 _____

FAMILY MEMBER #2 _____

VERB THAT ENDS IN -ING _____

A DIFFERENT FOOD _____

The Perfect Picnic Spot

Use the words from the previous page to complete a silly story.

When my family suggested having our lunch at the Cottonwood campground, I

was _____. I love eating my _____ outside! I knew we had picked up a
     EMOTION   FOOD

box of _____ from the _____ for after lunch, my favorite. We drove up
   SOMETHING SWEET   STORE

to the area and I jumped out of the _____. "I will find the perfect spot for
                  MODE OF TRANSPORTATION

a picnic!" I grabbed a _____ for us to sit on, and I ran off. I passed a picnic
         NOUN

table, but it was covered with _____ so we couldn't sit there. The next
           SOMETHING ALIVE

picnic table looked okay, but there were smears of _____ and pieces of
                  SAUCE

_____ everywhere. The people that were there before must have been
PLURAL VEGETABLES

_____! I gritted my _____ together and kept walking down the path,
ADJECTIVE   PLURAL BODY PART

determined to find the perfect spot. I wanted a table with a good view of the

trees. Why was this so hard? If we were lucky, I might even get to see _____
                         ANIMAL

eating some _____ on the cliffside. They don't have those in _____ where I
   PLURAL FRUIT   PLACE

am from. I walked down a little hill and there it was, the perfect spot! The trees

towered overhead and looked as tall as _____. The patch of grass was a
                SOMETHING TALL

beautiful _____ color. The _____ flowers were growing on
     COLOR   ADJECTIVE

the side of a _____. I looked across the prairie and even saw a _____
    NOUN   DIFFERENT ANIMAL

on the edge of a rock. I looked back to see my _____ and _____
                 FAMILY MEMBER #1 FAMILY MEMBER #2

_____ a picnic basket. "I hope you brought plenty of _____, I'm
VERB THAT ENDS IN ING   A DIFFERENT FOOD

starving!"

Hike to a Canyon

start here

DID YOU KNOW?
The Painted Canyon Trail, located in the South Unit of the park is a great way to get up close with the rock formations!

Theodore Roosevelt Word Search

Before becoming the 26th President of the United States, Theodore Roosevelt spent many years in the badlands of North Dakota hunting bison and learning about western life. His time there greatly influenced his later environmental efforts. He is remembered with a national park to honor his legacy of conservation.

1. President
2. Rancher
3. Naturalist
4. Father
5. Rough Rider
6. Colonel
7. leader
8. glasses
9. hunting
10. writing
11. Sagamore Hill
12. Harvard
13. Bull Moose
14. great
15. adventure
16. Medora

```
N W I L N C O L O N E L O W K
H A B U L L M O O S E R W G J
T R T R A R O D E M L B A L B
S O P U S P R U C E P L U A C
C U A I R E H C N A R S J S L
A G L D Y A O O D B E E A S I
R H A D R R L G A M S S I E N
P R B A M E I I G W I S K S G
R I R S G E L O S E D A S P M
E D I C A B O Y H T E L O T A
Q E A H A W R I T I N G N G N
S R N I K E O I S M T K I R E
I J O S H U N T I N G A Q E D
J Y G T L E V E S O O R V A O
N S A G A M O R E H I L L T M
X F T F A R E G L Z E S Q N E
U A L E A D E R N E T P V E B
C J A D V E N T U R E A L A S
```

31

Leave No Trace Quiz

Leave No Trace is a concept that helps people make decisions during outdoor recreation that protects the environment. There are seven principles that guide us when we spend time outdoors, whether you are in a national park or not. Are you an expert in Leave No Trace? Take this quiz and find out!

1. How can you plan ahead and prepare to ensure you have the best experience you can in the national park?
    a. Make sure you stop by the ranger station for a map and to ask about current conditions.
    b. Just wing it! You will know the best trail when you see it.
    c. Stick to your plan, even if conditions change. You traveled a long way to get here, and you should stick to your plan.
2. What is an example of traveling on a durable surface?
    a. Walking only on the designated path.
    b. Walking on the grass that borders the trail if the trail is very muddy.
    c. Taking a shortcut if you can find one since it means you will be walking less.
3. Why should you dispose of waste properly?
    a. You don't need to. Park rangers love to pick up the trash you leave behind.
    b. You actually should leave your leftovers behind, because animals will eat them. It is important to make sure they aren't hungry.
    c. So that other peoples' experiences of the park are not impacted by you leaving your waste behind.
4. How can you best follow the concept "leave what you find"?
    a. Take only a small rock or leaf to remember your trip.
    b. Take pictures, but leave any physical items where they are.
    c. Leave everything you find, unless it may be rare like an arrowhead, then it is okay to take.
5. What is not a good example of minimizing campfire impacts?
    a. Only having a campfire in a pre-existing campfire ring.
    b. Checking in with current conditions when you consider making a campfire.
    c. Building a new campfire ring in a location that has a better view.
6. What is a poor example of respecting wildlife?
    a. Building squirrel houses out of rocks so the squirrels have a place to live.
    b. Stay far away from wildlife and give them plenty of space.
    c. Reminding your grown-ups to not drive too fast in animal habitats while visiting the park.
7. How can you show consideration of other visitors?
    a. Play music on your speaker so other people at the campground can enjoy it.
    b. Wear headphones on the trail if you choose to listen to music.
    c. Make sure to yell "Hello!" to every animal you see at top volume.

Park Poetry

America's parks inspire art of all kinds. Painters, sculptors, photographers, writers, and artists of all mediums have taken inspiration from natural beauty. They have turned their inspiration into great works.

Use this space to write your own poem about the park. Think about what you have experienced or seen. Use descriptive language to create an acrostic poem. This type of poem has the first letter of each line spell out another word. Create an acrostic that spells out the word "Bison."

B _____

I _____

S _____

O _____

N _____

B irds

I nteresting fossils

S o much grass

O range sunsets

N ew adventure

B ig rocks

I n the dirt

S tories told

O pen skies

N ature all around

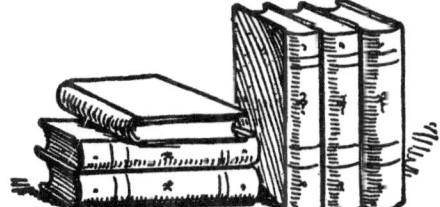

Take a Hike

Go for a hike with your friends or family. If you aren't able to visit Theodore Roosevelt National Park, go for a walk in a park near where you live. Read through the prompts before your walk and finish the activities after you return.

Draw something you saw that moves:

Draw something you saw when you looked up:

Draw something you saw that grows out of the ground:

Draw a picture of your favorite part of the walk:

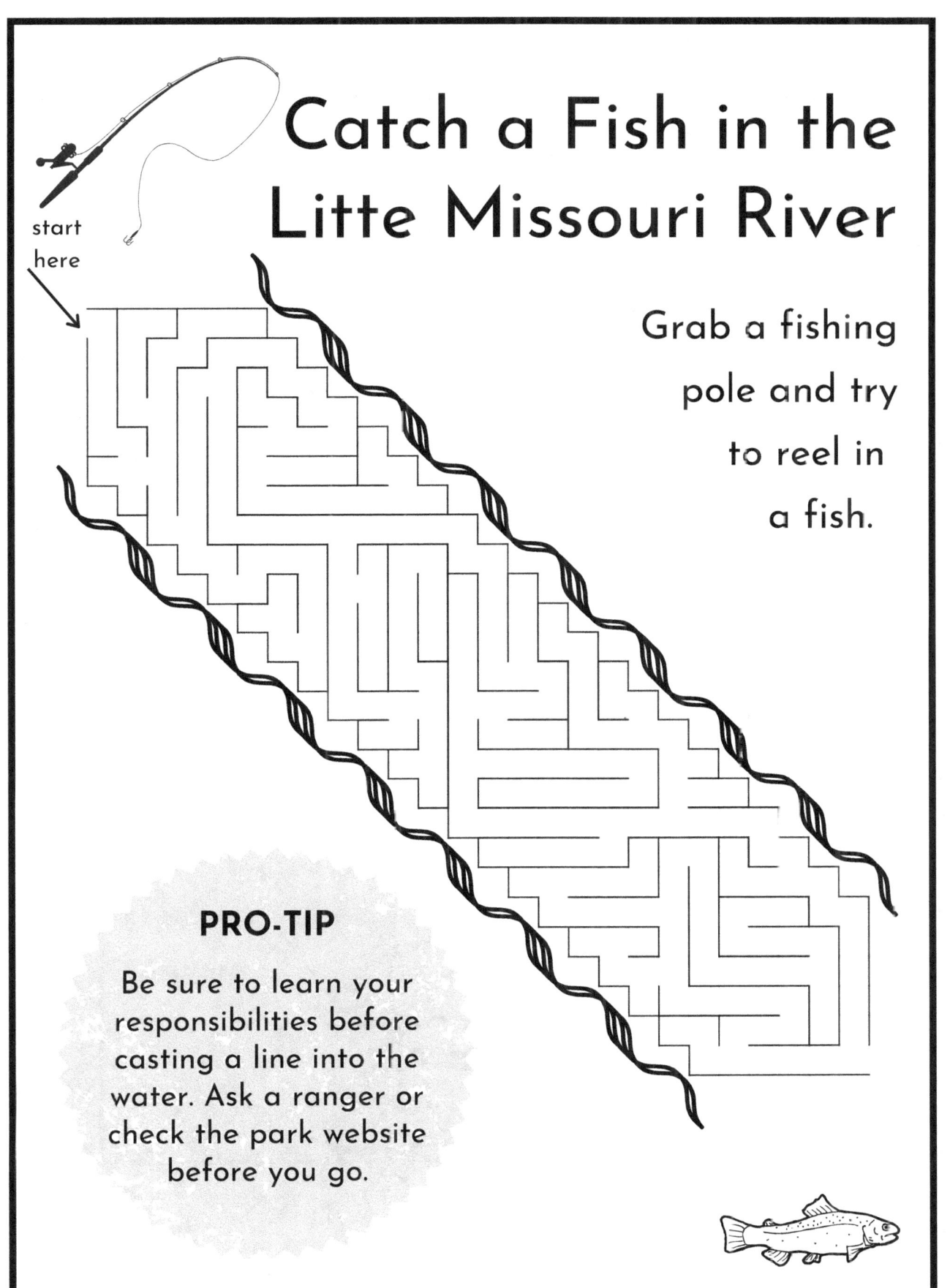

Catch a Fish in the Litte Missouri River

start here

Grab a fishing pole and try to reel in a fish.

PRO-TIP

Be sure to learn your responsibilities before casting a line into the water. Ask a ranger or check the park website before you go.

Stacking Rocks

Have you ever seen stacks of rocks while hiking in national parks? Do you know what they are or what they mean? These rock piles are called cairns and often mark hiking routes in parks. Every park has a different way to maintain trails and cairns. However, they all have the same rule: If you come across a cairn, do not disturb it.

Color the cairn and the rules to remember.

1. Do not tamper with cairns.

If a cairn is tampered with or an unauthorized one is built, then future visitors may become disoriented or even lost.

2. Do not build unauthorized cairns.

Moving rocks disturbs the soil and makes the area more prone to erosion. Disturbing rocks can disturb fragile plants.

3. Do not add to existing cairns.

Authorized cairns are carefully designed. Adding to them can actually cause them to collapse.

Decoding Using American Sign Language

American Sign Language, also called ASL for short, is a language that many Deaf people or people who are hard of hearing use to communicate. People use ASL to communicate with their hands. Did you know people from all over the country and world travel to national parks? You may hear people speaking other languages. You might also see people using ASL. Use the American Manual Alphabet chart to decode some national parks facts.

This was the first national park to be established:

__ __ __ __ __ __ __ __ __ __

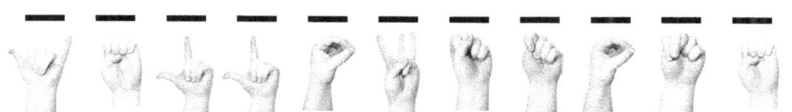

This is the biggest national park in the US:

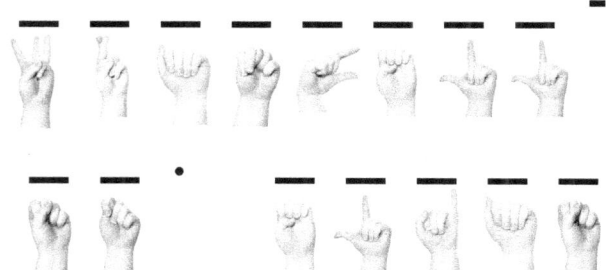

This is the most visited national park:

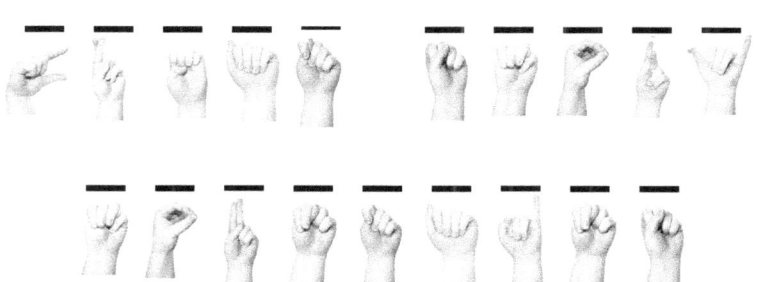

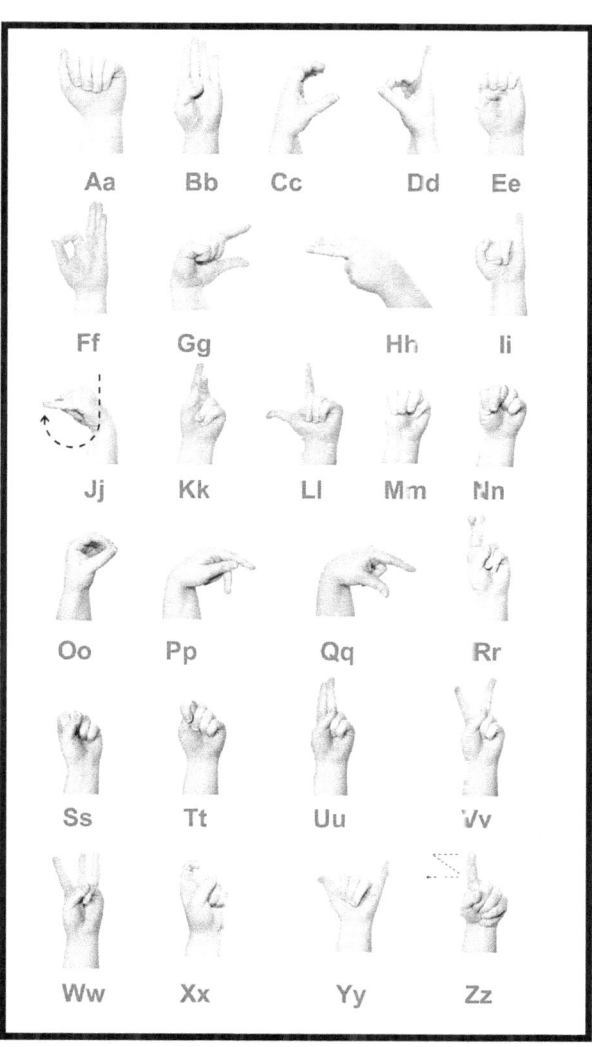

Hint: Pay close attention to the position of the thumb!

 Try it! Using the chart, try to make the letters of the alphabet with your hand. What is the hardest letter to make? Can you spell out your name? Show a friend or family member and have them watch you spell out the name of the national park you are in.

Go Birdwatching at The Big Plateau

start here

DID YOU KNOW?
Theodore Roosevelt National Park is home to several birds of prey, including eagles, hawks, and owls. Birds of prey are birds that hunt other animals for food.

Butterflies in the Prairie

Dozens of species of butterflies and moths live in Theodore Roosevelt National Park. Their wingspan size varies, as do the patterns on their wings. Design your butterfly below. Make sure the wings are symmetrical, meaning both sides match.

A Hike at Skyline Vista

Fill in the blanks on this page without looking at the full story. Once you have each line filled out, use the words you've chosen to complete the story on the next page.

ADJECTIVE _____

SOMETHING TO EAT _____

SOMETHING TO DRINK _____

NOUN _____

ARTICLE OF CLOTHING _____

BODY PART _____

VERB _____

ANIMAL _____

SAME TYPE OF FOOD _____

ADJECTIVE _____

SAME ANIMAL _____

VERB THAT ENDS IN "ED" _____

NUMBER _____

A DIFFERENT NUMBER _____

SOMETHING THAT FLIES _____

LIGHT SOURCE _____

PLURAL NOUN _____

FAMILY MEMBER _____

YOUR NICKNAME _____

A Hike at Skyline Vista

Use the words from the previous page to complete a silly story.

I went for a hike at Skyline Vista today. In my favorite _ _ _ _ _ _ _ backpack, I
ADJECTIVE

made sure to pack a map so I wouldn't get lost. I also threw in an extra

_ _ _ _ _ _ _ _ _ _ just in case I got hungry and a bottle of _ _ _ _ _ _ _ _ _ _ I put
SOMETHING TO EAT   SOMETHING TO DRINK

on my _ _ _ _ _ _ _ _ _ spray, and a tied a _ _ _ _ _ _ _ _ _ _ _ around my
NOUN   ARTICLE OF CLOTHING

_ _ _ _ _ _ _ _ _ _, in case it gets chilly. I started to _ _ _ _ _ _ down the path. As
BODY PART   VERB

soon as I turned the corner, I came face to face with a(n) _ _ _ _ _ _ _ _ _. I think
ANIMAL

it was as startled as I was! What should I do? I had to think fast! Should I

give it some of my _ _ _ _ _ _ _ _ _ _ _? No. I had to remember what the
SAME TYPE OF FOOD

_ _ _ _ _ _ _ ranger told me. "If you see one, back away slowly and try not to
ADJECTIVE

scare it." Soon enough, the _ _ _ _ _ _ _ _ _ _ _ _ _ _ _ _ _ _ _ away. The coast
SAME ANIMAL   VERB THAT ENDS IN ED

was clear. _ _ _ _ _ _ hours later, I finally got to the lookout. I felt like I could
NUMBER

see for a _ _ _ _ _ _ miles. I took a picture of a _ _ _ _ _ _ _ _ so I could always
A DIFFERENT NUMBER   NOUN

remember this moment. As I was putting my camera away, a _ _ _ _ _ _ _ _ _
SOMETHING THAT FLIES

flew by, reminding me that it was almost nighttime. I turned on my

_ _ _ _ _ _ _ _ _ _ and headed back. I could hear the _ _ _ _ _ _ _ _ _ _ singing their
LIGHT SOURCE   PLURAL INSECT

evening song. Just as I was getting tired, I saw my _ _ _ _ _ _ _ _ _ _ and our tent.
FAMILY MEMBER

"Welcome back _ _ _ _ _ _ _ _! How was your hike?"
NICKNAME

Design a Water Bottle

Imagine you've been hired to design a reusable water bottle that will be for sale in the South Unit Visitor Center. It will be a souvenir for visitors to remember their trip to the park and to North Dakota.

Consider adding a plant or animal that lives here, or include a famous place in the park or activity that you can do while visiting.

Cottonwood Campground
Word Search

Words may be horizontal, vertical, or diagonal and they might be backward!

1. tent
2. camp stove
3. sleeping bag
4. bug spray
5. sunscreen
6. map
7. flashlight
8. pillow
9. lantern
10. ice
11. snacks
12. smores
13. water
14. first aid kit
15. chair
16. cards
17. books
18. games
19. trail
20. hat

```
D P P I L L O W D B T E A C I
E O A D P R E A A M B R C A N
P W C A M P S T O V E I H X G
R A H S G E L E B E E D A P S
E L B U G S P R A Y N G I E A
S I A H G C I C N N M E R C N
C W N L A F I R S K O O B F K
M T A E M I L E L H M R W L J
T A P R E A O R E S L B A A B
S M P A S R R T E N T L U S C
C E A I I R C G P E I U J H A
S S N A C K S S I M O K I L R
I J R S F O I S N J R A Q I D
C Y E T L E V E G U O R V G S
E W T A K C A B B S S O H H M
X J N F I R S T A I D K I T T
U A A E S S E N G E T P V A B
C J L I A R T D N A M A H A S
```

All in the Day of a Park Ranger

Park Rangers are hardworking individuals dedicated to protecting our parks, monuments, museums, and more. They take care of the natural and cultural resources for future generations. Rangers also help protect the visitors of the park. Their responsibilities are broad and they work both with the public and behind the scenes.

What have you seen park rangers do? Use your knowledge of the duties of park rangers to fill out a typical daily schedule, one activity for each hour. Feel free to make up your own, but some examples of activities are provided on the right. Read carefully, not all of the example activities are befitting a ranger!

Time	Activity		Examples
6 am	Lead a sunrise hike		• feed the bald eagles
7 am			• build trails for visitors to enjoy
8 am			• throw rocks off the side of the mountain
9 am			• rescue lost hikers
10 am			• study animal behavior
11 am			• record air quality data
12 pm	Enjoy a lunch break outside		• answer questions at the visitor center
1 pm			• pick wildflowers
2 pm			• pick up litter
3 pm			• share marshmallows with squirrels
4 pm	Teach visitors about the geology of the badlands		• repair handrails
5 pm			• lead a class on a field trip
6 pm			• catch frogs and make them race
7 pm			• lead people on educational hikes
8 pm			• write articles for the park website
9 pm			• protect the river from pollution

Additional examples:
• remove non-native plants from the park
• study how climate change is affecting the park
• give a talk about prairie dogs
• lead a program for campers on the night skies

If you were a park ranger, which of the above tasks would you enjoy most?

_____

_____

Draw Yourself as a National Park Ranger

RANGER
_____

The Fish of Theodore Roosevelt NP

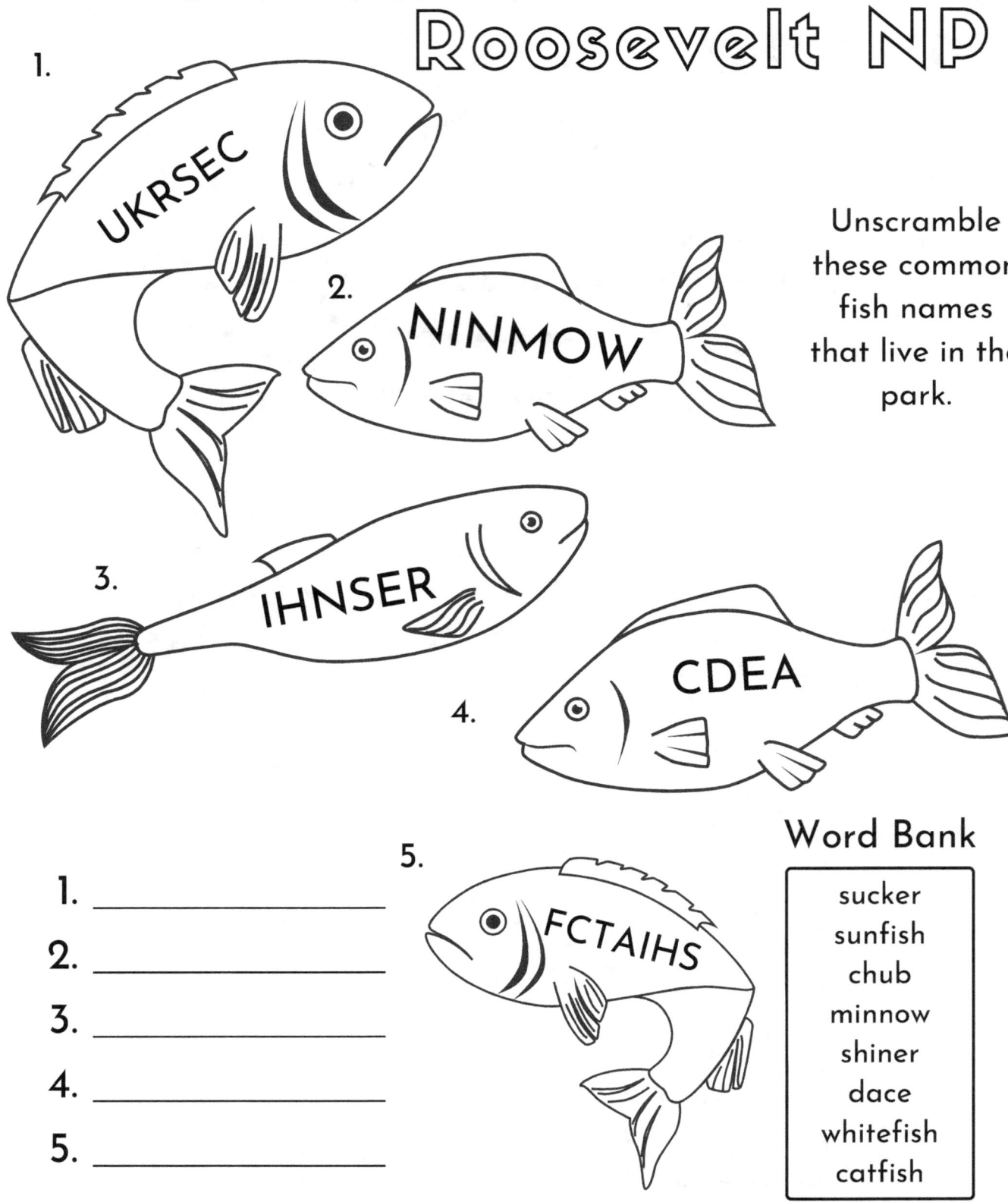

Unscramble these common fish names that live in the park.

1. UKRSEC

2. NINMOW

3. IHNSER

4. CDEA

5. FCTAIHS

1. _____
2. _____
3. _____
4. _____
5. _____

Word Bank

sucker
sunfish
chub
minnow
shiner
dace
whitefish
catfish

Amphibians

Three species of toad and two species of frogs live in Theodore Roosevelt Park. One type of salamander lives there too. Frogs and toads both spend the beginning of their lives the same way, as tadpoles. Tadpoles hatch from eggs in water, usually in springs or pools of water.

Both frogs and toads are amphibians. Salamanders are amphibians too. Color the amphibians below.

Sound Exploration

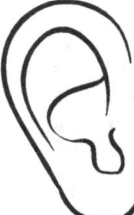 

Spend a minute or two listening to all of the sounds around you.
Draw your favorite sound.

How did this sound make you feel?

_____

_____

What did you think when you heard this sound?

_____

_____

Map Symbol Sudoku

The National Park System makes park maps using symbols instead of words.
They are easily understood and take up way less space on a tiny map.

Trailhead

Cabin

Wildlife

Campground

Complete this symbol sudoku puzzle. Fill each square with one of the symbols. Each one can appear only once in each row, column, and mini 2x2 grid. Each symbol means something, so you can write what the symbol represents instead of drawing the symbols if you prefer.

63 National Parks

How many other national parks have you been to? Which one do you want to visit next? Note that some of these parks fall on the border of more than one state, you may check it off more than once!

Alaska
- [ ] Denali National Park
- [ ] Gates of the Arctic National Park
- [ ] Glacier Bay National Park
- [ ] Katmai National Park
- [ ] Kenai Fjords National Park
- [ ] Kobuk Valley National Park
- [ ] Lake Clark National Park
- [ ] Wrangell-St. Elias National Park

American Samoa
- [ ] National Park of American Samoa

Arizona
- [ ] Grand Canyon National Park
- [ ] Petrified Forest National Park
- [ ] Saguaro National Park

Arkansas
- [ ] Hot Springs National Park

California
- [ ] Channel Islands National Park
- [ ] Death Valley National Park
- [ ] Joshua Tree National Park
- [ ] Kings Canyon National Park
- [ ] Lassen Volcanic National Park
- [ ] Pinnacles National Park
- [ ] Redwood National Park
- [ ] Sequoia National Park
- [ ] Yosemite National Park

Colorado
- [ ] Black Canyon of the Gunnison National Park
- [ ] Great Sand Dunes National Park
- [ ] Mesa Verde National Park
- [ ] Rocky Mountain National Park

Florida
- [ ] Biscayne National Park
- [ ] Dry Tortugas National Park
- [ ] Everglades National Park

Hawaii
- [ ] Haleakalā National Park
- [ ] Hawai'i Volcanoes National Park

Idaho
- [ ] Yellowstone National Park

Kentucky
- [ ] Mammoth Cave National Park

Indiana
- [ ] Indiana Dunes National Park

Maine
- [ ] Acadia National Park

Michigan
- [ ] Isle Royale National Park

Minnesota
- [ ] Voyageurs National Park

Missouri
- [ ] Gateway Arch National Park

Montana
- [ ] Glacier National Park
- [ ] Yellowstone National Park

Nevada
- [ ] Death Valley National Park
- [ ] Great Basin National Park

New Mexico
- [ ] Carlsbad Caverns National Park
- [ ] White Sands National Park

North Dakota
- [ ] Theodore Roosevelt National Park

North Carolina
- [ ] Great Smoky Mountains National Park

Ohio
- [ ] Cuyahoga Valley National Park

Oregon
- [ ] Crater Lake National Park

South Carolina
- [ ] Congaree National Park

South Dakota
- [ ] Badlands National Park
- [ ] Wind Cave National Park

Tennessee
- [ ] Great Smoky Mountains National Park

Texas
- [ ] Big Bend National Park
- [ ] Guadalupe Mountains National Park

Utah
- [ ] Arches National Park
- [ ] Bryce Canyon National Park
- [ ] Canyonlands National Park
- [ ] Capitol Reef National Park
- [ ] Zion National Park

Virgin Islands
- [ ] Virgin Islands National Park

Virginia
- [ ] Shenandoah National Park

Washington
- [ ] Mount Rainier National Park
- [ ] North Cascades National Park
- [ ] Olympic National Park

West Virginia
- [ ] New River Gorge National Park

Wyoming
- [ ] Grand Teton National Park
- [ ] Yellowstone National Park

Other National Parks

Besides Theodore Roosevelt National Park, there are 62 other diverse and beautifu national parks across the United States. Try your hand at this crossword. If you need help, look at the previous page for some hints.

Down

1. State where Acadia National Park is located
2. This national park has the Spanish word for turtle in it.
3. Number of national parks in Alaska
5. This national park has some of the hottes- temperatures in the world.
6. This national park is the only one in Idaho.
7. This toothsome creature can be famously found in Everglades National Park.
8. Only president with a national park named for them

Across

4. This state has the most national parks.
9. This park has some of the newest land in the US, caused by volcanic eruptions.
10. This park has the deepest ake in the Un ted States.
11. This color shows up in the rame of a national park in California.
12. This national park deserves a gold medal.

Which National Park Will You Go to Next?
Word Search

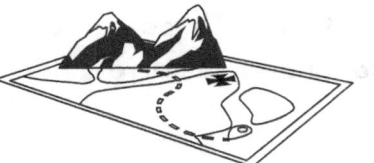

1. Zion
2. Big Bend
3. Glacier
4. Olympic
5. Sequoia
6. Bryce
7. Mesa Verde
8. Biscayne
9. Wind Cave
10. Great Basin
11. Katmai
12. Yellowstone
13. Voyageurs
14. Arches
15. Badlands
16. Denali
17. Glacier Bay
18. Hot Springs

```
F M M E S A V E R D E B N E Y
E A B I G B E N D E S A S E M
Y L I C A L O Y N E E D L T G
D M G A S S A U C N R L U E R
C E L I I T S C R E O A A K E
S N A W Y E E O I W T N A C A
G I C H A A Q C S E M D N S T
N O I Z P R U T I M R S N E B
I W E L M P O N B W E B K H A
R J R F D N I F L I H B U C S
P A B E E S A N E S O P W R I
S J A E N Y A C S I B A U A N
T C Y I A D O H H Y M E A L R
O T A T L M L E S E G R W R J
H S T O I K A T M A I R O P B
I C H U R C O L Y M P I C O U
O Y G T S D E O S B R Y C E T
W I N D C A V E I N R O H E M
```

52

Field Notes

Spend some time to reflect on your trip to Theodore Roosevelt National Park. Your field notes will help you remember the things you experienced. Use the space below to write about your day.

While I was at Theodore Roosevelt National Park...

I saw:
_____
_____
_____
_____

I heard:
_____
_____
_____

I felt:
_____

Draw a picture of your favorite thing in the park.

_____

I wondered:
_____
_____
_____
_____
_____

ANSWER KEY

Go Horseback Riding on the Jones Creek Trail

Help find the horse's lost shoe!

start here →

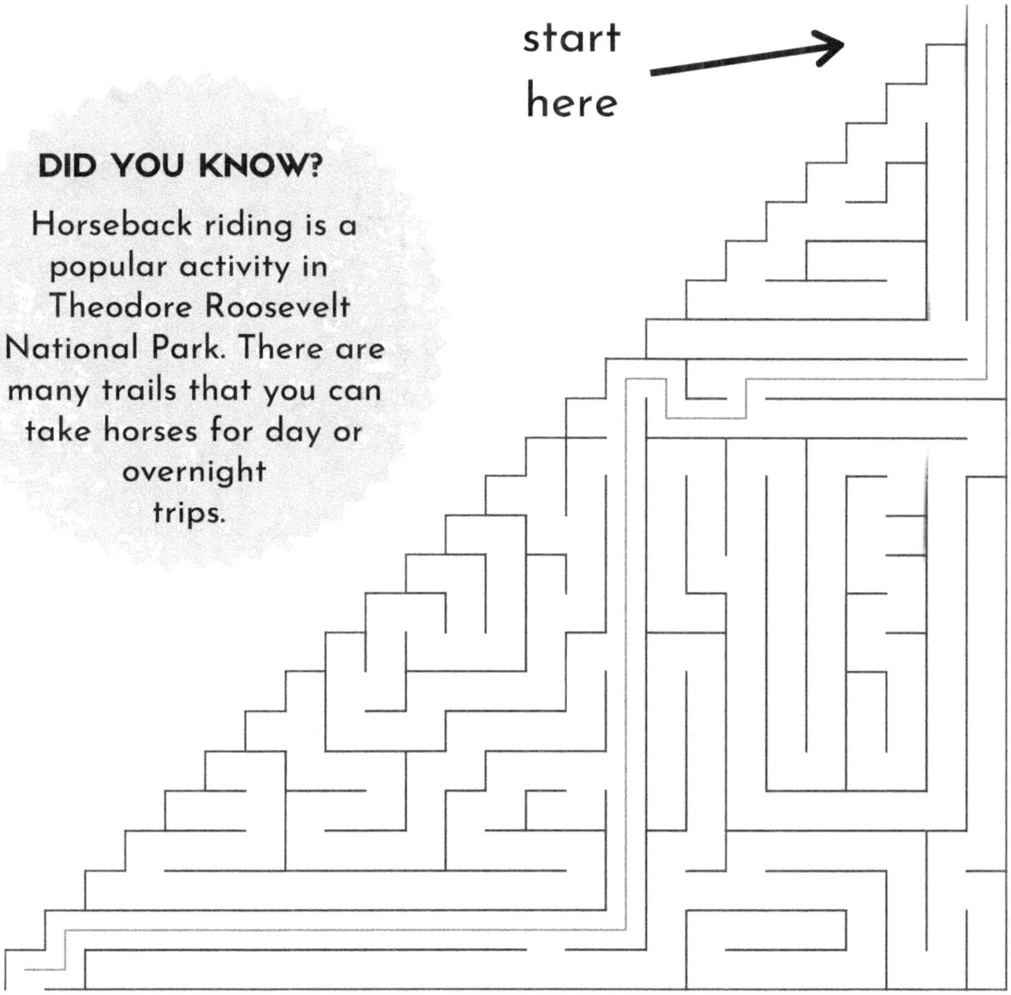

DID YOU KNOW?

Horseback riding is a popular activity in Theodore Roosevelt National Park. There are many trails that you can take horses for day or overnight trips.

Answers: Who lives here?

Here are nine plants and animals that live in the park.
Use the word bank to fill in the clues below.

PRAI**R**IE ■ DOG

PRONGH**O**RN

COY**O**TE

BI**S**ON

RATTL**E**SNAKE

POISON ■ **I** V Y

E LK

SA**L**AMANDER

WILD ■ **T** URKEY

Find the Match!
Common Names and Latin Names

Match the common name to the scientific name for each animal. The first one is done for you. Use clues on the page before and after this one to complete the matches.

Pronghorn   Haliaeetus leucocephalus

Water Plantain   Ovis canadensis

Plains Bluegrass   Picoides villosus

Bighorn Sheep   Mustela nigripes

Great Horned Owl   Alisma triviale

Bald Eagle   Crotalus viridis

Hairy Woodpecker   Bubo virginianus

Black-footed Ferret   Antilcapra americana

Prairie Rattlesnake   Poa arida

Bald Eagle

Haliaeetus leucocephalus

Jumbles Answers

1. FISHING

2. BIRDING

3. CAMPING

4. PICNICKING

5. SIGHTSEEING

6. STAR GAZING

National Park Emblem Answers

1. This represents all plants. **Sequoia Tree**

2. This represents all animals. **Bison**

3. This symbol represents the landscapes. **Mountains**

4. This represents the waters protected by the park service. **Water**

5. This represents the historical and archeological values. **Arrowhead**

Answers: The Ten Essentials

The ten essentials is a list of things that are important to have when you go for longer hikes. If you go on a hike to the <u>backcountry</u>, it is especially important that you have everything you need in case of an emergency. If you get lost or something unforeseen happens, it is good to be prepared to survive until help finds you.

The ten essentials list was developed in the 1930s by an outdoors group called the Mountaineers. Over time and technological advancements, this list has evolved. Can you identify all the things on the current list? Circle each of the "essentials" and cross out everything that doesn't make the cut.

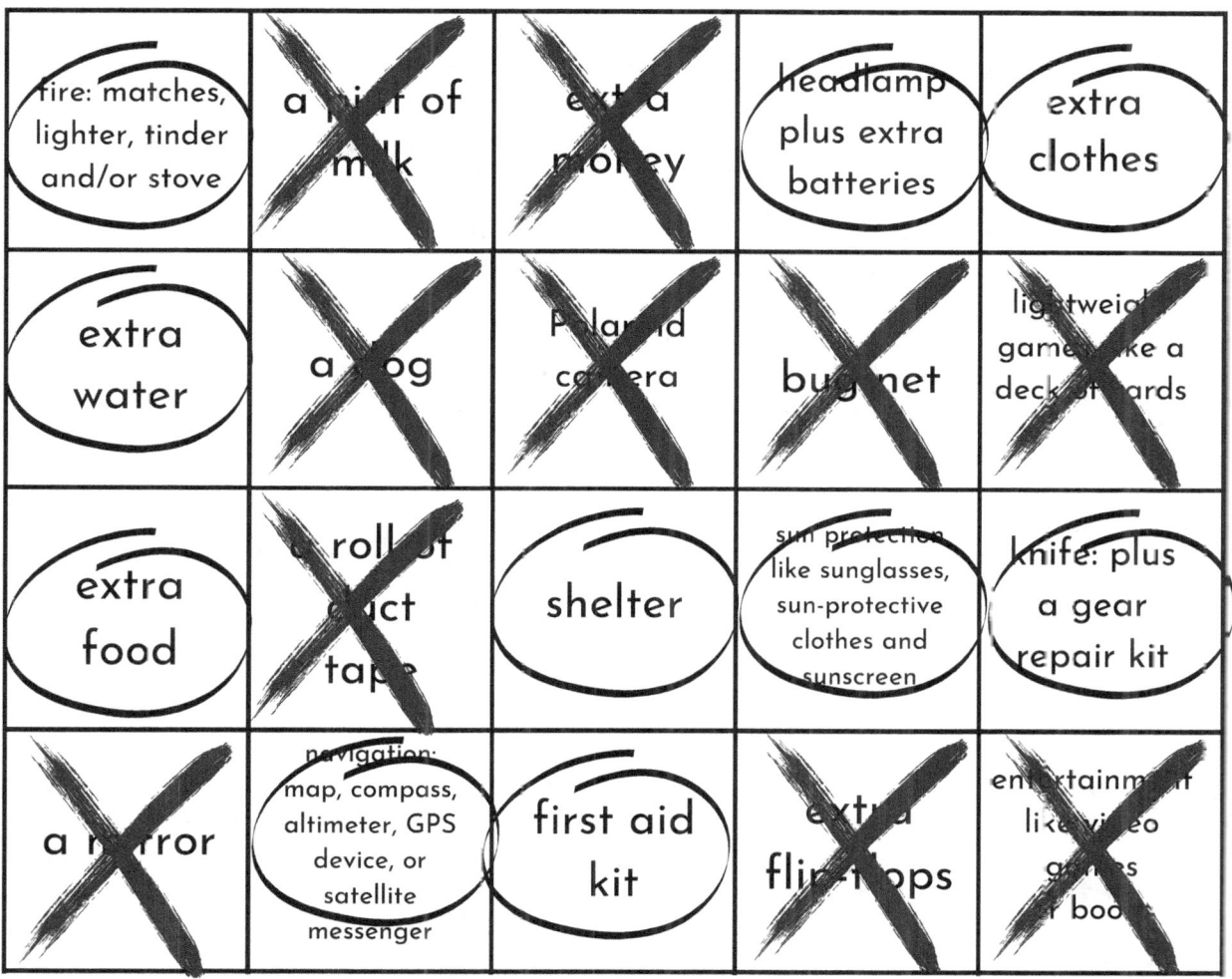

Backcountry- a remote undeveloped rural area.

Theodore Roosevelt Word Search

Words may be horizontal, vertical, or diagonal
and they might be backward!

1. bison
2. badlands
3. Teddy
4. North Dakota
5. ranch
6. cabin
7. horse
8. rattlesnakes
9. Peck Hill
10. conservation
11. camp ground
12. prairie dogs
13. oil boom
14. maltese
15. sagebrush
16. snapping turtle

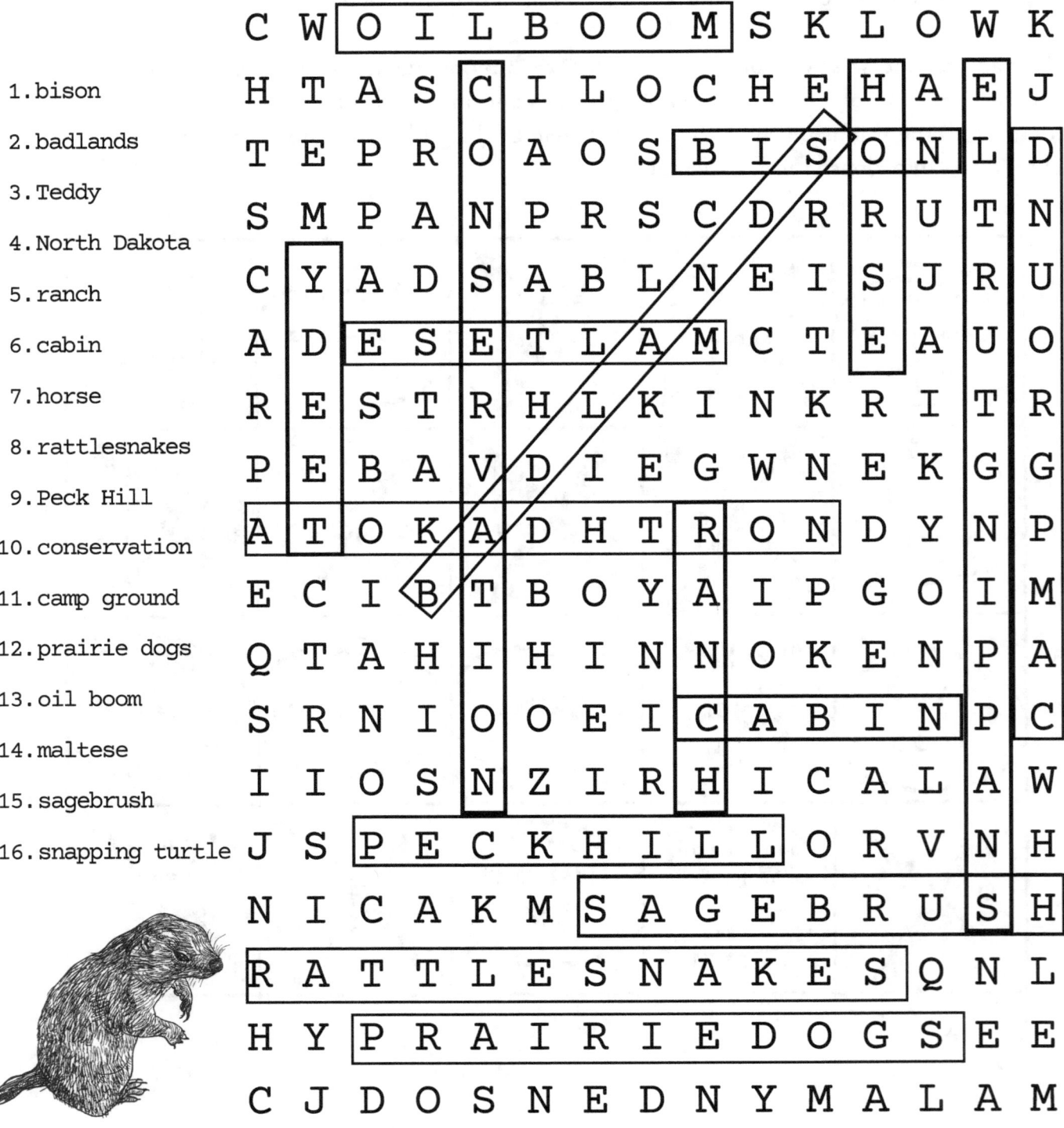

```
C W O I L B O O M S K L O W K
H T A S C I L O C H E H A E J
T E P R O A O S B I S O N L D
S M P A N P R S C D R R U T N
C Y A D S A B L N E I S J R U
A D E S E T L A M C T E A U O
R E S T R H L K I N K R I T R
P E B A V D I E G W N E K G G
A T O K A D H T R O N D Y N P
E C I B T B O Y A I P G O I M
Q T A H I H I N N O K E N P A
S R N I O O E I C A B I N P C
I I O S N Z I R H I C A L A W
J S P E C K H I L L O R V N H
N I C A K M S A G E B R U S H
R A T T L E S N A K E S Q N L
H Y P R A I R I E D O G S E E
C J D O S N E D N Y M A L A M
```

Wildlife Wisdom

The national park is home to a lot of different kinds of animals. Seeing wildlife can be an exciting thing about visiting the national park but it is important to remember that these animals are wild. They need plenty of space and a healthy habitat where they can find their own food. Part of this is not allowing animals to eat any human food. This is their home and we are the visitors. We need to be respectful of the wildlife in the park.

Directions: Circle the highlighted words that best complete the following sentences.

If an animal changes its behavior because of your presence, you are:
A) too close
B) funny looking
C) dehydrated and should drink more water

The best thing we can do to help wild animals survive is:
A) make them pets
B) protect their habitat
C) knit them winter sweaters

In a national park, it is okay to share your food with wild animals:
A) never
B) always
C) sometimes

When you're hiking in an area where there are bears, you should warn bears that you are entering their space by:
A) hiking quietly
B) making noise
C) wearing bright colors

At night, park rangers care for the animals by:
A) putting them back into their cages
B) tucking them into bed
C) leaving them alone

If you see an abandoned bird's nest, it is best to:
A) pet the baby birds
B) leave it alone
C) crunch the empty eggshells

Bears look under logs in hopes of finding:
A) granola bars
B) insects
C) peanuts to eat

The place where an animal lives is called its
A) condo
B) habitat
C) crib

Solution: Hike to a Canyon

DID YOU KNOW?
The Painted Canyon trail, located in the South Unit of the park is a great way to get up close with the rock formations!

Theodore Roosevelt Themed Word Search

Before becoming the 26th President of the United States, Theodore Roosevelt spent many years in the badlands of North Dakota hunting bison and learning about western life. His time there greatly influenced his later environmental efforts. He is remembered with a national park to honor his legacy of conservation.

1. President
2. Rancher
3. Naturalist
4. Father
5. Rough Rider
6. Colonel
7. leader
8. glasses
9. hunting
10. writing
11. Sagamore Hill
12. Harvard
13. Bull Moose
14. great
15. adventure
16. Medora

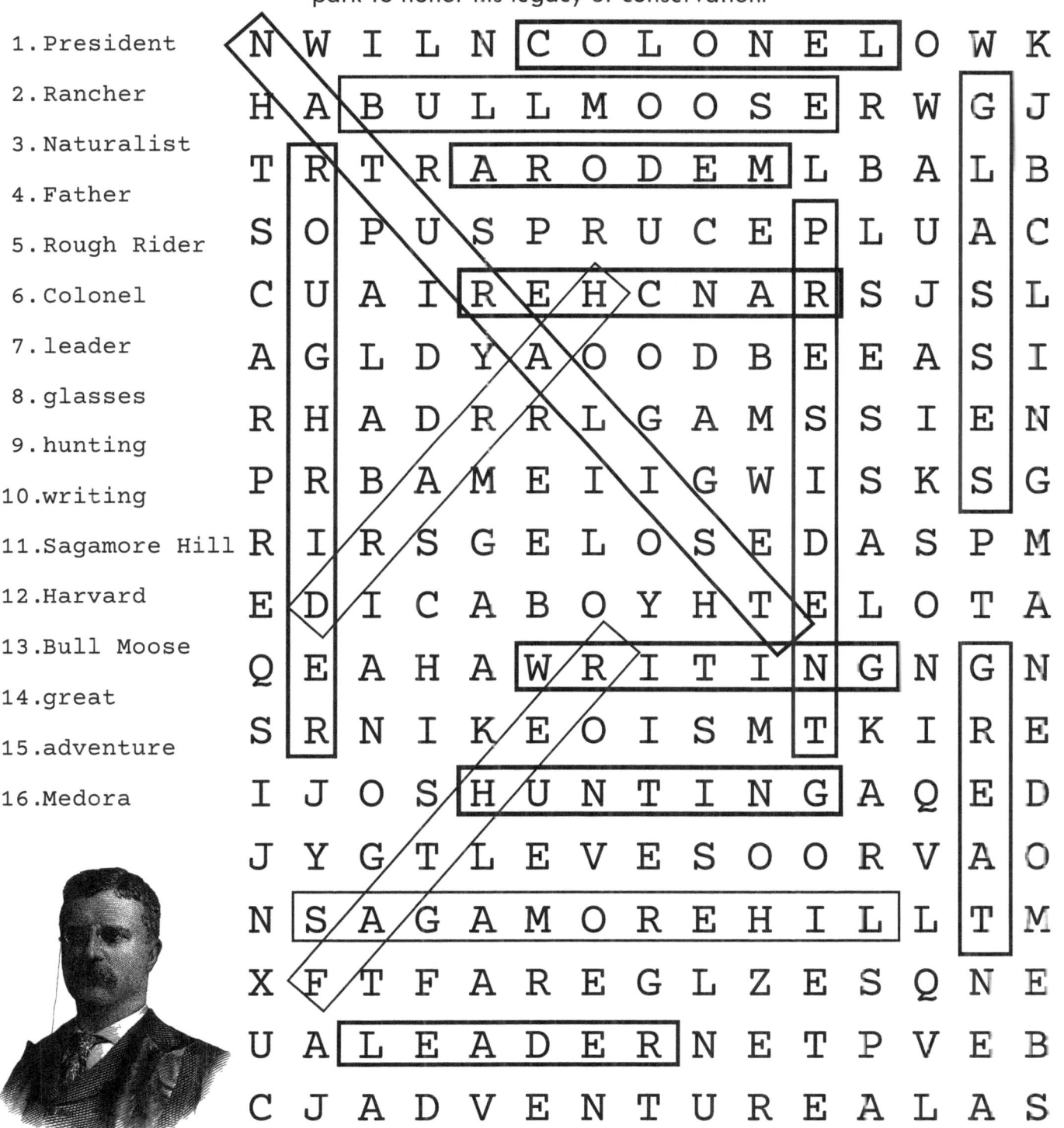

```
N W I L N C O L O N E L O W K
H A B U L L M O O S E R W G J
T R T R A R O D E M L B A L B
S O P U S P R U C E P L U A C
C U A I R E H C N A R S J S L
A G L D Y A O O D B E E A S I
R H A D R R L G A M S S I E N
P R B A M E I I G W I S K S G
R I R S G E L O S E D A S P M
E D I C A B O Y H T E L O T A
Q E A H A W R I T I N G N G N
S R N I K E O I S M T K I R E
I J O S H U N T I N G A Q E D
J Y G T L E V E S O O R V A O
N S A G A M O R E H I L L T M
X F T F A R E G L Z E S Q N E
U A L E A D E R N E T P V E B
C J A D V E N T U R E A L A S
```

63

Answers: Leave No Trace Quiz

Leave No Trace is a concept that helps people make decisions during outdoor recreation that protects the environment. There are seven principles that guide us when we spend time outdoors, whether you are in a national park or not. Are you an expert in Leave No Trace? Take this quiz and find out!

1. How can you plan ahead and prepare to ensure you have the best experience you can in the National Park?

    A. Make sure you stop by the ranger station for a map and to ask about current conditions.

2. What is an example of traveling on a durable surface?

    A. Walking only on the designated path.

3. Why should you dispose of waste properly?

    C. So that other peoples' experiences of the park are not impacted by you leaving your waste behind.

4. How can you best follow the concept "leave what you find"?

    B. Take pictures but leave any physical items where they are.

5. What is not a good example of minimizing campfire impacts?

    C. Building a new campfire ring in a location that has a better view.

6. What is a poor example of respecting wildlife?

    A. Building squirrel houses out of rocks from the river so the squirrels have a place to live.

7. How can you show consideration of other visitors?

    B. Wear headphones on the trail if you choose to listen to music.

Solution: Catch a Fish in the Litte Missouri River

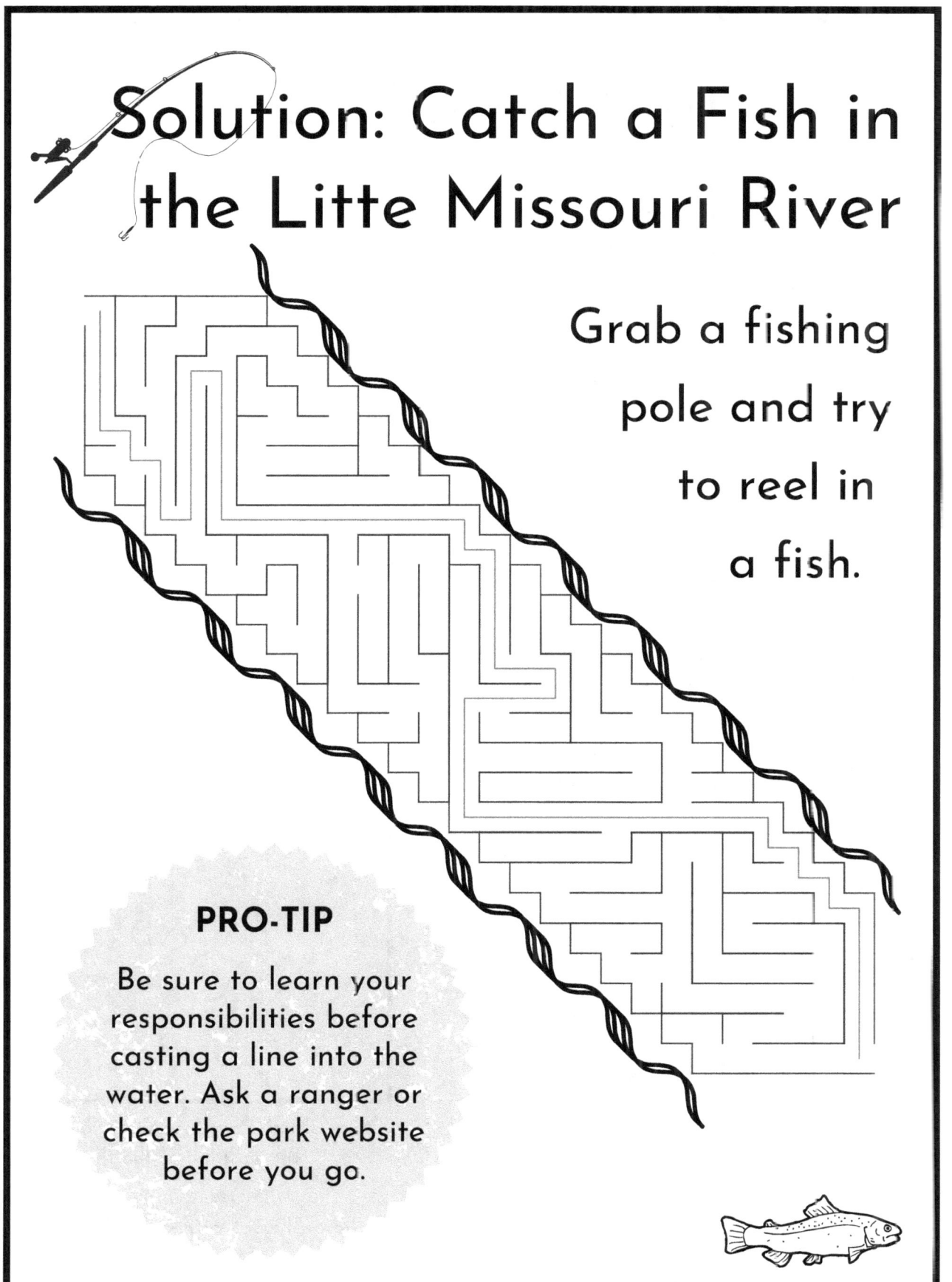

Grab a fishing pole and try to reel in a fish.

PRO-TIP

Be sure to learn your responsibilities before casting a line into the water. Ask a ranger or check the park website before you go.

Decoding Using American Sign Language

American Sign Language, also called ASL for short, is a language that many Deaf people or people who are hard of hearing use to communicate. People use ASL to communicate with their hands. Did you know people from all over the country and world travel to national parks? You may hear people speaking other languages. You might also see people using ASL. Use the American Manual Alphabet chart to decode some national parks facts.

This was the first national park to be established:

Y E L L O W S T O N E
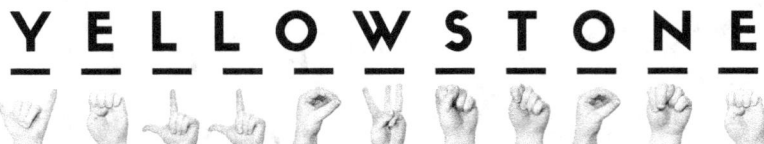

This is the biggest national park in the US:

W R A N G E L L -
S T . E L I A S

This is the most visited national park:

G R E A T S M O K Y
M O U N T A I N S

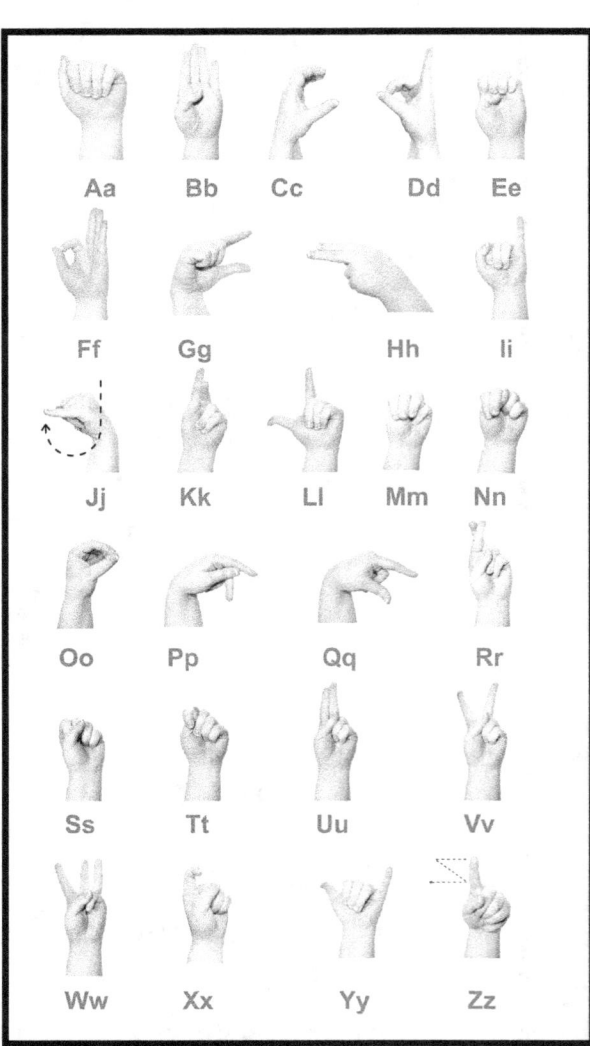

Hint: Pay close attention to the position of the thumb!

Try it! Using the chart, try to make the letters of the alphabet with your hand. What is the hardest letter to make? Can you spell out your name? Show a friend or family member and have them watch you spell out the name of the national park you are in.

Solution: Go Birdwatching at The Big Plateau

start here

DID YOU KNOW?
Theodore Roosevelt NP is home to several birds of prey, including eagles, hawks, and owls. Birds of prey are birds that hunt other animals for food.

Cottonwood Campground
Word Search

1. tent
2. camp stove
3. sleeping bag
4. bug spray
5. sunscreen
6. map
7. flashlight
8. pillow
9. lantern
10. ice
11. snacks
12. smores
13. water
14. first aid kit
15. chair
16. cards
17. books
18. games
19. trail
20. hat

D P P I L L O W D B T E A C I
E O A D P R E A A M B R C A N
P W C A M P S T O V E I H X G
R A H S G E L E B E E D A P S
E L B U G S P R A Y N G I E A
S I A H G C I C N N M E R C N
C W N L A F I R S K O O B F K
M T A E M I L E L H M R W L J
T A P R E A O R E S L B A A B
S M P A S R R T E N T L U S C
C E A I I R C G P E I U J H A
S S N A C K S S I M O K I L R
I J R S F O I S N J R A Q I D
C Y E T L E V E G U O R V G S
E W T A K C A B B S S O H H M
X J N F I R S T A I D K I T T
U A A E S S E N G E T P V A B
C J L I A R T D N A M A H A S

The Fish of Theodore Roosevelt National Park

1.   SUCKER
2.   MINNOW
3.   SHINER
4.   DACE
5.   CATFISH

Map Symbol Sudoku Anwers

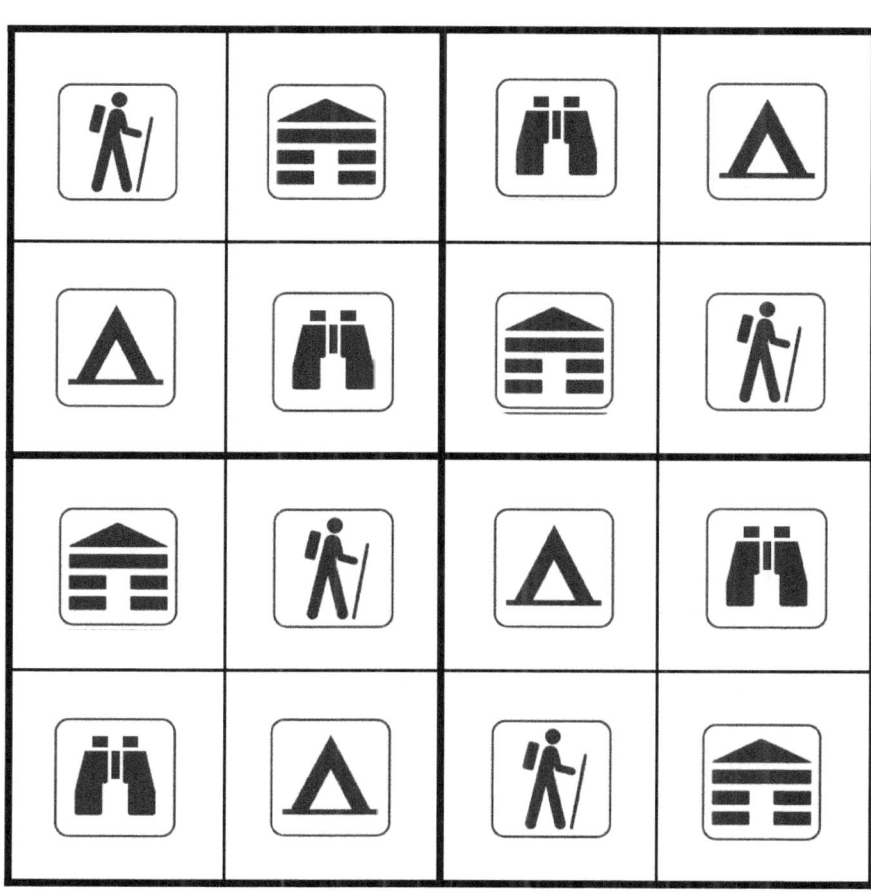

Answers: Other National Parks

Down

1. State where Acadia National Park is located
2. This National Park has the Spanish word for turtle in it
3. Number of National Parks in Alaska
5. This National Park has some of the hottest temperatures in the world
6. This National Park is the only one in Idaho
7. This toothsome creature can be famously found in Everglades National Park
8. Only president with a national park named for them

Across

4. This state has the most National Parks
9. This park has some of the newest land in the US, caused by a volcanic eruption
10. This park has the deepest lake in the United States
11. This color shows up in the name of a National Park in California
12. This National Park deserves a gold medal

Answers: Where National Park Will You Go Next?

1. Zion
2. Big Bend
3. Glacier
4. Olympic
5. Sequoia
6. Bryce
7. Mesa Verde
8. Biscayne
9. Wind Cave
10. Great Basin
11. Katmai
12. Yellowstone
13. Voyageurs
14. Arches
15. Badlands
16. Denali
17. Glacier Bay
18. Hot Springs

Little Bison Press is an independent children's book publisher based in the Pacific Northwest. We promote exploration, conservation, and adventure through our books. Established in 2021, our passion for outside spaces and travel inspired the creation of Little Bison Press.

We seek to publish books that support children in learning about and caring for the natural places in our world.

To learn more, visit:
LittleBisonPress.com

Want more free games and activities? Visit our website!